For Lovers of
BIRDS

EDWARD LEAR

Compiled by
Vivien Noakes &
Charles Lewsen

COLLINS
ST JAMES'S PLACE, LONDON
1978

William Collins Sons and Co Ltd
London · Glasgow · Sydney · Auckland
Toronto · Johannesburg

First published in 1978
© Vivien Noakes and Charles Lewson 1978
ISBN 0 00 222038 5
Set in 10 on 12 point Ehrhardt
Made and Printed litho in Great Britain
by W & J Mackay Ltd, Chatham

Introduction

All his life Edward Lear hated noise, yet at the age of eighteen he set himself to work in the Parrot House at London Zoo. For nearly two years in that squawking bedlam he made painstaking drawings for *Illustrations of the Family of Psittacidae*, a book of Parrots which is now recognised as one of the masterpieces of ornithological illustration. He illustrated other bird books, but his sight began to fail so that when he was twenty-five he lamented, "no bird under an ostrich shall I soon be able to see to do." He became a landscape painter, but he never lost that earlier skill, and he filled his Nonsense world with birds – birds like no other birds, birds like people and people like birds. With his large round spectacles, Lear appeared to others as well as to himself like a benign owl.

In the last year of his life, Lear wrote to a friend: "My ten pigeons are a great amusement, & their punctual ways – 2 hours exactly on their eggs – & then 2 hours at liberty are very curious. Giuseppi Orsini my servant (says he) believes they have little watches under their wings, & that they wind them up at 7 pm – holding them with one foot & turning the key with t'other." "I must stop. The pigeons & roses are desirable & pleasant facts."

O Brother Chicken! Sister Chick!
   O gracious me! O my!
This broken Eggshell was my home!
   I see it with my eye!
However did I get inside?
   Or how did I get out?
And must my life be evermore,
      an atmosphere of doubt?

Can no one tell? Can no one solve,
   This mystery of Eggs?
Or why we chirp & flap our wings, –
   or why we've all 2 legs?
And since we cannot understand, —
   May it not seem to me,
That we are merely born by chance,
   Egg-nostics for to be?

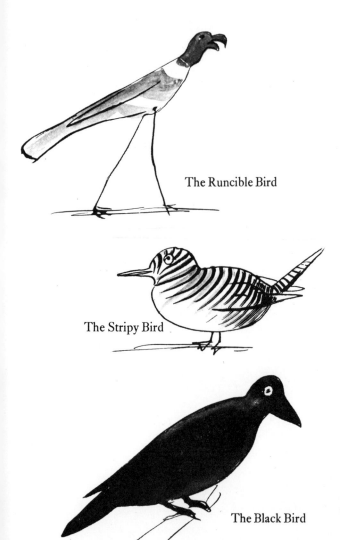

The Runcible Bird

The Stripy Bird

The Black Bird

The Scroobious Bird

The Spotty Bird

The Gray Bird

There was a Young Lady whose bonnet
Came untied when the birds sate upon it;
But she said, "I don't care! all the birds in the air
Are welcome to sit on my bonnet!"

The Visibly Vicious Vulture,
who wrote some Verses to a
Veal-cutlet in a Volume
bound in Vellum.

The Perpendicular Purple Polly,
who read the Newspaper and ate Parsnip-Pie
with his Spectacles.

There was an Old Man with a beard,
Who said, "It is just as I feared! ——
Two Owls and a Hen, four Larks and a Wren,
Have all built their nests in my beard!"

Owls are plentiful. Flights of grey gregarious gaggling grisogorous geese adorn the silver shining surface of the softly sounding sea.

In the morning I feed unfortunate birds.

Why are the little birds melancholy at sunrise?
Because their little bills are all over dew ? due ?

There was an Old Man on whose nose,
Most birds of the air could repose;
But they all flew away at the closing of day,
Which relieved that Old Man and his nose.

The Pelican Chorus

King and Queen of the Pelicans we;
No other Birds so grand we see!
None but we have feet like fins!
With lovely leathery throats and chins!
    Ploffskin, Pluffskin, Pelican jee!
    We think no birds so happy as we!
    Plumpskin, Ploshkin, Pelican jill!
    We think so then, and we thought so still!

We live on the Nile. The Nile we love.
By night we sleep on the cliffs above;
By day we fish, and at eve we stand
On long bare islands of yellow sand.
And when the sun sinks slowly down
And the great rock walls grow dark and brown,
Where the purple river rolls fast and dim
And the Ivory Ibis starlike skim,
Wing to wing we dance around, ——
Stamping our feet with a flumpy sound, ——
Opening our mouths as Pelicans ought,
And this is the song we nightly snort; ——
    Ploffskin, Pluffskin, Pelican jee, ——
    We think no Birds so happy as we!
    Plumpskin, Ploshkin, Pelican jill,——
    We think so then, and we thought so still.

Last year came out our Daughter, Dell;
And all the Birds received her well.
To do her honour, a feast we made
For every bird that can swim or wade.
Herons and Gulls, and Cormorants black,
Cranes, and Flamingoes with scarlet back,
Plovers and Storks, and Geese in clouds,
Swans and Dilberry Ducks in crowds.
Thousands of Birds in wondrous flight!
They ate and drank and danced all night,
And echoing back from the rocks you heard
Multitude-echoes from Bird and Bird, ——
    Ploffskin, Pluffskin, Pelican jee,
    We think no Birds so happy as we!
    Plumpskin, Ploshkin, Pelican jill,
    We think so then, and we thought so still!

Yes, they came; and among the rest,
The King of the Cranes all grandly dressed.
Such a lovely tail! Its feathers float
Between the ends of his blue dress-coat;
With pea-green trowsers all so neat,
And a delicate frill to hide his feet, ——
(For though no one speaks of it, every one knows,
He has got no webs between his toes!)

As soon as he saw our Daughter Dell,
In violent love that Crane King fell, ——
On seeing her waddling form so fair,
With a wreath of shrimps in her short white hair.
And before the end of the next long day,
Our Dell had given her heart away;
For the King of the Cranes had won that heart,
With a Crocodile's egg and a large fish-tart.
She vowed to marry the King of the Cranes,
Leaving the Nile for stranger plains;
And away they flew in a gathering crowd
Of endless birds in a lengthening cloud.
    Ploffskin, Pluffskin, Pelican jee,
    We think no birds so happy as we!
    Plumpskin, Ploshkin, Pelican jill,
    We think so then, and we thought so still!

And far away in the twilight sky,
We heard them singing a lessening cry, ——
Farther and farther till out of sight,
And we stood alone in the silent night!
Often since, in the nights of June,
We sit on the sand and watch the moon; ——
She has gone to the great Gromboolian plain,
And we probably never shall meet again!
Oft, in the long still nights of June,
We sit on the rocks and watch the moon; –
—————— She dwells by the streams of the Chankly Bore,
And we probably never shall see her more.

   Ploffskin, Pluffskin, Pelican jee,
   We think no Birds so happy as we!
   Plumpskin, Ploshkin, Pelican jill,
   We think so then, and we thought so still!

The Chancellor – (I was there Saturday & Sunday –)
was delightful: such an abundance of excellent con-
versation – with a circle, or with me only —— one
seldom has the luck of getting.

He, – Speaking of "undique sequaces" ——— &
"sequax", —— & saying, —— "let us remember
the line & go & look for the translation" quoth the
Landscape painter in a fit of absurdity –

"My Lord I can remember it easily by thinking
of wild ducks."

—— "How of wild Ducks Lear?" —— said
the Lord C. —— "Because they are *sea-quacks*"
said I.

"Lear" – said his Lordship "I abominate the
forcible introduction of ridiculous images calculated
to distract the mind from what it is contemplating."

Here & there are bits of desert sand with a few palms, & some of that poisonous euphorbia. A few geese or ducks now & then in the still water – with ever a long necked Heron peering to keep watch, & informing the more busy ducks, who pay him in fishes for his assistance in saving their lives.

Mrs. Blue Dickey-bird, who went out a-walking
with her six chickey birds: she carried a parasol
and wore a bonnet of green silk.
The first little chickey bird had daisies growing out
of his head, and wore boots because of the dirt.
The second little chickey bird wore a hat, for fear it
should rain.
The third little chickey bird carried a jug of water.
The fourth little chickey bird carried a muff, to keep
her wings warm.
The fifth little chickey bird was round as a ball.
And the sixth little chickey bird walked on his head,
to save his feet.

Calico Pie,
The Little Birds fly
Down to the calico tree,
Their wings were blue,
And they sang "Tilly-loo!"
And they never came back to me!
    They never came back!
    They never came back!
They never came back to me!

Acknowledgements

*For permission to reproduce material
in this book we are grateful to :*
Colonel W. R. Prescott
The Houghton Library, Harvard University
The Tennyson Research Centre, Lincoln, by courtesy of
Lord Tennyson and the Lincolnshire Library Service
The Master and Fellows of Balliol College, Oxford
The Trustees of the National Portrait Gallery
The Somerset Record Office
The Robert H. Taylor Collection, Princeton University
The Victoria & Albert Museum
and to the Oxford University Press for whom
Vivien Noakes and Charles Lewsen are preparing
the definitive edition of Edward Lear's nonsense.

O! – that's enough about myself which I wish I was
a seagull & could fly off to Jaffa at once.